Merl & Patty
Thank you fo
Best Wish

The Gift
of the
Word

Robert R. Dimitroff

PublishAmerica
Baltimore

Robert R. Dimitroff

ISBN: 1-60563-876-5
PUBLISHED BY PUBLISHAMERICA, LLLP
www.publishamerica.com
Baltimore

Printed in the United States of America

In loving memory of
my grandmother,
my inspiration for this book.

A Happy Ending

Just a normal July day in Sommerset, Pa.

When nine miners went to work in the usual way

But something happened when they drilled the wall

Water poured in and they started to fall

Trapped 240 feet, Oh, could they be saved?

Or would they be entombed in a watery grave

Above the ground the workers tried

To reach the men before they died

Trouble came when a drill bit broke

They continued to work and never gave up hope

Then on the third day families and wives

Got the miracle they wanted all nine were alive

For seventy-seven hours their fate was pending

Thank God he decided on a happy ending.

A River Runs Free

She flows through the mountains to the valley below

A constant reminder we don't know where it goes

The river is alive as it slowly goes by

The question stays unanswered and we just don't know why

Long and wide and so very deep

It looks so tranquil in its endless sleep

But no matter where we go or where we might be

We'll never learn why a river runs free.

A Silent World

In a life of silence most may feel fear

When you listen with your hands and not from the ear

The language used by deaf and mute

Is poetry in motion like the notes of a flute

Sometimes their emotions are so overlooked

But their history can be traced in volumes of books

From composer, author, and movie star

To Miss America they have come so far

So remember when you see their hands move with grace

They're not different for we are all a part of the human race

A Soldier's Farewell

I served my country and answered the call

And knew someday that I might fall.

I have an appointment I must keep

But I'll be in your dream each time you sleep

God called me home to take my place

To live for eternity in his loving embrace

So shed a tear and remember me well

For what happens in life no one can tell.

I fought the war and my battle is done

This is a soldier's farewell to everyone.

A Summer Evening

When God turns off his Heavenly light

He allows the stars to twinkle at night

Here at home the cool wind blows

It comes so quickly and then it goes

I sit on my front porch swinging

Admiring the beauty of a Summer evening

Now Mother Nature does her part

To show her splendor from the heart

The frogs croak and the crickets chirp

And all is peaceful here on earth

It is all part of the Master's plan

To create a picture with his hands

So when God finally stops his painting

He will call his portrait "A Summer Evening".

A Wife's Love

What is more precious than the stars above

That shines and twinkles at night and holds

A special place in your heart

When tears and heartaches start.

The one thing that will always be

As constant as new falling snow

And no matter how bad life may get

This will always show.

So enjoy your life and all it brings

From your wedding vows and your golden ring.

Because no matter how hard life may be

With all its strife

There's nothing that God made as special

As the love of a wife.

A World Without Song

Not a bird would be singing their sweet melody

Or the wind would be blowing in low harmony

The church bells would stop chiming on every Sunday morn.

And joyous refrain when a baby is born.

How could we survive, all would be wrong

If we had to live our life in a world without song.

And Then There Is One

Two men stand alone tonight

In the square arena ready to fight

When they ring the bell the battle begins

And all will watch eagerly to see how it ends.

Like gladiators they fight as sweat fills their eyes

They're angry and desperate as the punches fly

They do it for glory and to see who will win.

Then when it is over and the war is won

The victor's hand is raised and then there is one.

Autoworker

Around the nation you will find

Men and women working on the assembly line

They work their skill with precision and grace

You can tell they work hard by the sweat on their face

The job is not glamorous or the pay very high

They take pride in their work, and work hard to get by

So the next time you're driving a truck or a car

Think of the ones who helped you go far

For the autoworker has opened the door

That allows you to select a Chevy, Chrysler or Ford.

Autumn Leaves

The treetops drop tears into the breeze

We know them best as Autumn leaves.

Multi color with different shape & size

Their beauty and luster is hard to realize.

A heavenly portrait in Mother Nature's scheme

They illustrate a vision seen only in dreams.

They're here a short time and then we will grieve.

But thank God for the time that we see Autumn leaves.

Barber Shop

In a little town that's not too far

You can get there by bike or even a car

Stands an old brick building by a traffic light

With a candy cane pole, it's a beautiful sight

Walk through the door and you'll find a chair

So just take a seat and they'll cut your hair

A place where news and events unfold

With stories and secrets that shouldn't be told.

No other place in the world can be found

With the humming of clippers and hair all around

So if you need a trim or just a little off the top

Go see the barber at your local Barber Shop.

Bartender

In a busy city or a rural town

There is a lady who lays the whiskey down

With the skill and grace of an acrobat

She can make any drink for you exact

Some crowds are large and others small

But that doesn't matter, she serves them all

So remember her tip and she'll show you her splendor

For she is one of a kind, your Bartender.

Beauty of It All

Mother Nature awakens the leaves in the fall

And allows us to see the beauty of it all

Mountains arise at Gods beacon call

And we marvel at the beauty of it all.

No matter if you're a baby, or a man who stands tall

The world is here to admire the beauty of it all

So look around and remember what you saw

And praise God he allowed you to see the beauty of it all.

Best Friend

Through life's journey of endless roads

We all need someone to help shoulder the load

A special person sent from above

Full of goodness, strength, and a whole lot of love

Someone who never tells you goodbye

But is there to laugh with you and wipe your tears when you cry

The only one you tell secrets to

And when times get hard, they know what to do

Best friends may not always be husband and wife

It could be a brother or sister, someone dear in your life

So remember God's gift and how blessed you have been

To be able to be someone's best friend.

Big Bands

I remember the music of yesterday

The sweet sounds of Goodman, Miller, and Dorsey

How there was no room on the dance floor

As the Big Bands played during the Second World War

A time we spent by the radio

To hear news of the war and Bob Hope Show

In The Mood brought our spirits high

And Moon Light Serenade made us want to cry

Taking the A-Train or Chattanooga Choo Choo

In our minds, we knew we'd get through

Or listening to Sentimental Journey when the day was done

And who could forget Duke Ellington.

From Cab Calloway to Ella Fitzgerald

They are the ones who made life so grand

The music we loved played by The Big Bands.

Brother

We became close from the start

And swore we'd never grow apart

Through thick and thin there we were

I'd listen to big brother's every word

There were times that we would fight

But against someone else, we were always right

Now life slows down for no one

And the childish things we did were no longer fun

As years pass, so do the miles

Then so frequent are the smiles

For now, I'm married and a father

But I will always cherish the memories with my brother.

Butterflies Do Cry

When the sun goes down and the moon shines

And the flowers go to sleep

You can hear the sound of loneliness, if you try

Because Butterflies do cry.

When the wind blows loud and the air is cold

And the willow branches sway

You'll hear the familiar sound of sorrow and sigh

Because Butterflies do cry.

Chilling Tribute

A bugler plays in the chilly cold breeze

A reminder, a soldier has been knocked to his knees.

A tune so familiar when someone has died

For they served their Country and now here they lye.

Written by a fighter in the Civil War stand

And his father found the music in his dying son's hands.

Once you have heard it you will never forget

The chilling tribute I talk about is the anthem called Taps.

Daddy's Baby Girl

On that special day when love is true

And the world is in a whirl

The day a life starts anew

For Daddys Baby Girl.

The day she talks and takes a walk

And learns a few new thrills

She always smiles and laughs aloud

That's Daddys Baby Girl.

The years go by so, so fast

And time no longer lasts.

She will always be the jewel, the pearl,

That's Daddys Baby Girl.

Day the World Tumbled Down

On that gloomy September Day

Where lives were lost and we all prayed

Four Planes traveled to a destiny

With helpless souls who knew not why

Their trip would end and they would die.

But on the ground where Hero's came

To help the one's who had no name,

Through fire, smoke and broken dirt.

Some lost their lives and some were hurt

But at the end the world would cry,

Hug their families and wonder why,

Evil men who didn't care

Made the children lose their flair

Of a happy life without a frown

The day the world tumbled down.

Don't Go Away

Songs of love that make you sad

Bring two people together and they are glad

For love is a mystery so who can say

Why loved ones cry, "Don't go away".

Time stands still without a clue

Our lives are turned around and become blue

Some loves are precious and will never die

Other loves are never meant to be tried

But when the air blows and the trees sway

We hear someone whisper, "Don't go away".

Love is more than a four-letter word

That should be spoken often and constantly heard

So, hold on to life each passing day

And you will never have to say, "Don't go away".

Fame

From the beginning of time the story's been told

About something more precious than silver and gold.

All that search try to get a name

By finding this thing that we call Fame.

Some will pass and others fail

But the one's who lose will never tell

Of all their sorrow and their shame

Trying to find the thing called Fame.

If you are lucky and it comes your way

It may not last for more than a day

For 15 minutes is all we may get

To be someone we haven't yet.

It may not last for more than a day.

So be yourself for it's all a game

For you may never find this thing called Fame.

Family

Like drops of water in an endless sea

So are the generations of a family tree

From the beginning of time to every tomorrow

The family strives and continues to grow

They cover every country and nation on earth

The legacy continues with each passing birth

Families range from large to small

The history is something we all must recall

For whom we are or plan to be

All began with a branch from our family tree

So never, stop wondering about your past

For you and your children must make it last

A family is special and God made it so

So, be proud of your name wherever you go.

Final Flight

Once again down my face tears will stream

For we lost more Astronauts fulfilling their dream

Just like 1986 with the Challenger Seven

God called the Columbia crew to explore Heaven

On a clear February day while on their way back

Their shuttle exploded, reminding us of what we lack

Oh no! Not again, how could this be?

This cannot keep happening in the land of the free

But Anderson, Brown, Clark, Chawa, Husband, McCool, and Ramon

Cannot say what went wrong for they are all gone

One a doctor who gave his all

Three served in the military and answered the call

One's love for football could be seen on his face

Two came from other countries to help the space race

Now the universe remains for us to explore

So in their memory we must continue forever more

Fish

A life that's spent in a world of water

They swim carefree without a bother

Multicolor, they look so cool

And we know they're smart for they stay in schools

Large ones, small ones, skinny or fat

We fry them in a pan because we like them like that.

If they could talk and have one wish

They would say, "Let me stay in the water and not on your dish".

Gift of the Word

A blank piece of paper with a ballpoint pen,

Waiting for thoughts where no thought have been.

My head starts spinning with many words,

Making me wonder will they ever be heard.

Suddenly something happens that I can't control,

My hand starts to move and the words start to flow.

Oh what magic I can feel it appear,

Letters on paper that will always endure.

Lord you have blessed me, and I give you the glory,

By letting me express thoughts in the form of a story.

Some of the sweetest language I ever heard,

Thank you Dear Jesus for the Gift of the Word.

God Said

If I wake in the morning or die in my bed

It's all because God said.

The air that I breathe is not mine to keep

Or the tears that fall every time I weep.

These things are given for a price that was paid

Jesus shed his blood on the cross because God said.

So hold your family and give them a kiss

For if you take this for granted you would be remiss.

For all we have or will ever see

Is because the Lord our God said it would be.

God's Gift to Me

On a warm Spring Day in the month of May

Beside an Apple Tree

I saw your face and knew that day

You were God's gift to me.

As months and days and hours passed

Our life so fancy free

I look at you and know it's true

You are God's gift to me.

So as we journey through our new life,

With a love that can only be

Between the one's whose eyes can see

Forever and ever you will always be

God's Gift To Me.

Goodbye

When the sun sets and the moon rises high

That is the daylights way of saying goodbye

A sad reminder that nothing will last

Goodbye is a word that turns present to past

A happy word when we go for a ride

A sad word when someone has died

It has many faces this two-syllable word

It brings sadness to children whenever heard

Authors, poets, family and friends

Use this word to tell you the end

But do not be discouraged or even cry

Just because someone leaves, it's not always goodbye.

Graduate

The years of schooling have made you wise

And you see life's journey through different eyes

Now you walk the stage to a new tomorrow

With lots of dreams and a little sorrow

The memories will never go

You'll always remember the happy times and friends you know

Family was there when you needed them most

To love and support you no matter the cost

So, this is the time to celebrate

For this is the day, you graduate.

Grandfather

His hands are rough as leather

With a grip as hard as steel

He's the trunk of our tree of life

That stands strong and always will

Through his life came many changes

That we read about in books

And he's lived them all though some he can't recall

He will tell you what he knows

As the years go by and I think back

Of the man who changed my life

How he faced adversity and took it all in strife

My grandfather was a legend to those of us he knew

He made the world a better place

For his heart was always true.

Grandmother

Wrinkled hands with a gentle touch

And years of wisdom that means so much

She is not very tall but she is not pouting

With her heart of gold, she is as tall as a mountain

The cornerstone of a generation

A life full of hope and inspiration

Her legacy will always be alive and well

Through the lives of her loved ones and the stories they tell

And when God finally calls her home

We will always remember the love she has shown.

He Called Me Home

It happened today, he called me home

My journey was over I need not roam

I heard his voice so soft and sweet

I knew it was time for my Lord to meet.

Two angels came and took my hand

In an instance I was in the Promise Land

Then I saw my Savior's face

Full of kindness, love and grace.

He spoke to me so meek and mild

He said, "Welcome home my precious child"

Now I live in a mansion on high

For he called me home the moment I died.

He Had a Dream

He had a dream that we would live

Together, forever with love to give.

He had a dream we would do what is right

As brothers and sisters, black and white.

He had a dream that the Civil Rights War

Would end with freedom for all wealthy and poor.

He had a dream that education for the young

Would bring children together showing segregation is wrong.

In Washington D.C., he gave a speech

For millions of people his voice would reach.

But in Memphis, Tennessee, a shot was heard

That would end his life and silence his word.

So in his memory we must take his place

For Dr. Martin Luther King, Jr. had a dream for the whole human race.

He Was the Man

In a black Chevrolet with a big number three

He drove the raceway so fancy free

His birth name was Earnhardt but a few years later

The people would know him as the "Intimidator"

Feared by drivers, loved by fans

His legend lives on for he was the man

Now God felt the need to start a race

So he called on Dale to put it in place

Although he was taken to the Promise Land

There was never a doubt he was the man

Now Dale Jr. carries the flame

For his dad whose credentials was his name

When they wave the checkered flag from the stand

Dale looks down and remembers he was the man.

Heaven

Heaven is a place in the Bible, we're told

Where the streets are paved in solid gold

The Kingdom of God where mansions are made

For those who are saved and continue to pray

For Jesus died and shed his blood

So we can go to Heaven and be loved

Here on earth we dream of peace

Only Heaven can provide the true release

From pain and suffering and constant sorrow

We believe in Heaven for a better tomorrow

For God's word is written and his love is true

We know Heaven waits for me and you.

Hidden Scars

She is a woman, mother and beautiful wife

That just wants to live a simple life

For her dream there comes a cost

Years of abuse and a love that is lost

For the man she married so many years

Has shattered her spirit and brought her to tears

Why did she ever let it get this far?

Through her smile, she covers the hidden scars

Physical and mental abuse everyday

No one should have to live this way

For her children's sake, she tries to hold on

And prays for the time her abuser is gone

Then the day comes she finally gets strong

And realizes her hidden scars are all gone.

Homeless

They say in America we have a right to live free

But there are some people out there we refuse to see.

They suffer and struggle to survive everyday

And we choose to ignore them in our own selfish way.

We don't ask the reason and really care why

As long as we're happy we don't care if they die.

But we must stop the madness for this could happen to you

For fate has a way of stopping everything that we do.

So read your Bible and remember you're blessed

And work hard together to help the homeless.

How Did He Know?

He came to my house walking real slow

And began to tell a story in a voice real low

It sounded familiar and I got really scared

It was my life story that I'd never share.

Every detail, moment, and endless frame

Came out in an instant no matter the shame

He would not stop talking until I yelled "Please"

Then I cried and fell down on my knees

The only thing I could tell Him was "Go"

I never found out, "How did he know?"

In Memory Of

In Washington D.C., there is a Wall

With the names of loved ones who answered the call

Tall, dark marble, smooth to the touch

It is a solemn reminder of who gave so much

Husbands and sons went off to fight

Leaving wives and mothers to cry every night

War is hell, so we've been told

That's why it is meant for the brave and bold

Hero's are not born; they're made day by day

And we live to honor them in our own special way

So we build many statues and walls filled with love

So we'll always remember that they're in memory of.

Infantryman

His hands are rough and his face is scarred

A daily reminder of a life so hard

The years of fighting he gave up hope

Though the lonely nights he could not cope

Back at home a family waits

For some kind of word of their loved ones fate

When he finally comes home from his killing span

You see a grim reminder of the life of the Infantryman.

It Will Be Okay

Life is full of good times and bad

We sometimes overlook what we have

Family, friends, and a place to live

We seem to always have more than we give

Sometimes the waiting gets too hard

When you want something so bad, but it's not in the cards

Now patience is a virtue we don't like to use

For we feel, we have already paid our dues

Keep your head up, it will be ok

For tomorrow brings forward a brand new day.

Karaoke

Across the country in clubs and bars

There is some new entertainment that is not too far

It is called karaoke and it comes from Japan

You don't need a voice just a mike in your hand

For this is your chance to sing like a bird

You might not know the words; it's just something you heard

But don't you worry, just join the big scene

For the words will appear on a television screen

No matter the tune or how old it may be

Just look in the book and pick one that you see

So, stop staying at home and take out your wife

To a karaoke place and have the time of your life.

Land of the Brave

Our history is long and a traditional one

For it tells of all the heroics, we have done

From Washington to Lincoln and both World Wars

We never failed to open our doors

The whole world knows what we gave

That is why they all come to the land of the brave

There was a time we fought each other

Many a son was taken from their mother

Or the Civil Rights Battle that was fought over color

How sad it is to hate one another

But we awoke and got through the pain

And swore we would never let it happen again

Our country has flourished because freedom won't rave

So be thankful you live in the land of the brave.

Let the Children Pray

Throughout our nations claim to fame

We have never held our head in shame

Recently we have a lot to say

About how religion no longer pays

But if God ever turns his back

We will always be reminded of what we lack

For we are free and will remain that way

As long as we let the children pray

In the Bible, it is written how Jesus loved

And the children are precious to him like the dove

For they are life's great destiny

And will grow to keep our nation free

So, do not take them for granted or ever sway

Always take time to let the children pray.

Librarian

She comes to work with a special look

And spends her day checking out books

The job is not always a glorious one

But she works very hard until it is done

Working with kids at a computer desk

Keeping them quiet is quite a task

The Librarian goes through a daily routine

With a smile on her face when ever she's seen

So when you see her tell her you care

She'll always be there with book knowledge to share.

Life Goes On

When times seem hard and there is no hope

That's when we search deep for someway to cope

God never said every day would be fun

Just stop and remember life goes on.

No matter how bad we think life can be

There's always someone whose worse off then we

So, try to be happy for every day brings the sun

And always remember, life goes on.

Lighthouse

A Lighthouse shines it's glorious light

To bring all ships home safe at night

And when the sea won't set them free

She shines her light for all to see.

The lights have shown for many years

And saved sailors from a fear of dying

Leaving families back home crying.

So the ships sail with mercy on their side

For the lighthouse will always be their guide

When ships are lost their bells make a sound

So the lighthouse can guide them back to safe ground.

Not all vessels could be saved

They now lye in a watery grave

But for those who make it safe to shore

Is the reason she'll shine forever more.

Little Angel

Sleep precious angel your work is done

The battle you fought on earth is won.

Jesus has called you to his place

To live eternally in his grace.

Although families will cry because you died

There's peace ever after on the other side.

So spread your wings and start to sing

And we'll always remember the joy you bring.

We know on earth there's a better place

Where soon we'll be able to see your face

So go, Little Angel, and do your best

For we know you earned your eternal rest.

Love

As fragile as the pedals of a rose

This four-letter word that is sweet to the voice

Many have tried to understand love

A feeling from God sent down from above

So often misused or misunderstood

Some use it for evil and others for good

Oh what a feeling we all should be blessed

To be able to touch it in a hug or a kiss

But if we ever lose compassion

Love will never be in fashion

So like a spider whose web is woven

Catch all your feeling and never stop loving.

Memories

The river of life flows by fast

And all we have left is our past

Some days are good and some are sad

But most are the best we'll ever have

From childhood to adult life with all it's trails, hopes, and fears.

We keep hold of throughout the years.

So as children grow and grandchildren arrive

We tell them how we lived our lives.

With stories and old photographs

We try to relive our sacred past

The one thing we will cherish most

Are the memories that we haven't lost.

Mind of a Child

Fairy tales and story books

Some of the things that make children look

Through little eyes with mysterious glare

They make up stories that they love to share

An endless journey of learning and fun

In magical kingdoms as bright as the sun

But who can look into the mind of a child

With castles, dragons and crocodiles

They are the future so meek and mild

That's the mystery in the mind of a child.

Mommy's Smile

At the time of birth and life's new trials

The first thing we see is Mommy's smile.

As we grow up and learn to talk

We see Mommy's smile and to her we walk.

As we board the bus to go to school

We are so scared of the rules

But before we leave to drive the miles

We look out the window and see Mommy's smile.

But the years go by so very fast

And the time has come to leave at last

With hugs and kisses full of love

We leave the nest to try our best.

When days are long and nights are cold

We long for someone to have and to hold

So we sleep and dream a while

There we'll find Mommy's smile.

More than a Cloth

From the time that our country was born

We fought for freedom and sounded our horn

Our national emblem is red, white and blue

But sometimes we abuse it, so what can we do?

I will tell you, so listen close

Our American flag is more than a cloth

The stars represent the states we fought for

And the thirteen stripes for the colonies sworn

To fight for the rights of everyone

It makes me mad to see it abused

So if you're not sure, ask how it is used

Don't fly it torn or upside down

And never let it touch the ground

Take pride in your nation and let Old Glory fly

For many have protected it and some had to die

So remember, she's more than a cloth, she's America's pride.

My Younger Years

Looking back through my past

I realize it went by so fast

From childhood to becoming a man

There were so many things I didn't understand

Like "Why did I leave home at such an early age?"

To start a new chapter and turn one more page

I joined the service so I could be tough

But it was one journey that really was rough

The crazy things I did in my whirlwind life

Brought sorrow and heartache to my children and wife

Now as I grow older, I shed a tear

For I can't change my younger years.

Mystery of Life

From a babies cry at the time of birth

To the day of death when we return to the earth

We read and wonder what this secret could be

That keeps the mystery of life away from you and me

Many religions hope and pray

That God would tell them the answer someday

But neither sons or daughters, husbands or wives

Will ever discover the mystery of life.

Nations Protectors

In the big city or rural town

There is a special person that can be found

You might not see them every day

For they protect and defend in there own way

They make the streets safe for us at night

And allow you to sleep without a light

To children they are heroes in uniform

They have protected their rights from the day they were born

So often, we take their jobs for granted

And expect so much from them when we panic

So let us not forget our crime collectors

They are law enforcement, the nations protectors.

Ordinary

Life is filled with twisted roads

Every entrance and exit takes its toll

But if the load is too hard to carry

It just means that you are ordinary.

The secret of a happy life

May be found with a husband or wife

But if you find that so contrary

Don't worry, you're only ordinary.

Being ordinary is not so bad

It makes some people happy and others sad

But the world keeps turning round and round

And who knows where peace will be found

So relax, enjoy, be happy and merry

Because remember, you're only ordinary.

So be yourself and you'll go far

We can't all be a super star

For hopes and dreams, they all vary

Especially if you're ordinary.

Paratroopers Never Die

In nineteen hundred and forty one
World War II had just begun
We won the victories from the sky
Because Paratroopers never die.
In the Korean War we met a foe
Who did his fighting in the snow
We fought hard, with spirits high
Because Paratroopers never die.

In Vietnam, with jungles hot,
They tried to beat us, but they could not.
Airborne Troopers fought and raised the flag high
Because Paratroopers never die.
In Grenada, Panama, and Desert Storm,
And all the battles we have won
We set a standard for all to try
Because Paratroopers never die.

Back home, when my father passed,
A Paratrooper among the best,
I did not weep when he left,
Because I knew he passed the test
And now he's gone to be on high
With all the Paratroopers who never die.

Patience

In this world of toil and trouble

We feel we are always on the double

But just slow down and take a chance

For life is short, so have patience.

We as people are constantly on the go

And we are moving to where, we do not know

One day it will all stop in an instance

Then you will realize you should have had patience.

So up or down, forward or back

Just take your time and see what you lack

Remember every day will bring a brand new glance

To see this thing we call "Patience".

Pool Shark

With stick in hand he stands by a table

Waiting to play who ever feels able

He racks the balls and chalks the cue

Ready for the night to earn his just dues

Young or old it just does not matter

They all want to win to make their money belt fatter

In his eyes, there is always a spark

For no one can touch this man the pool shark.

Prison in My Mind

Words without letter and music without song

They're in my head where they just don't belong

Memories are darkness it makes me go blind

All this is captured in the prison in my mind.

It's hard to remember how far back I must go

To imagine the creatures locked deep in my soul

But it doesn't matter, it'll all be fine

For I have the key to the prison in my mind.

One day it'll be over and all that I seek

Shall be release of the prison and my thoughts will all freak.

So I wait for that moment when rest I shall find

When the walls have all tumbled around the prison in my mind.

Read Them and Weep

With a deck of cards and cold hard face

He walks to the table and then takes his place

No matter the game or if the ante's too steep

He'll look you straight in the eye and say read them and weep.

With the precision and skill he'll deal out your hand

And you can tell by his eyes that he is the man.

He plays all night long and when the sun rises high

He takes all your money and tells you good-bye.

So be very careful for the man who will creep

To your table and tell you to read them and weep.

Silver Wings

His daddy's stories could be told

About a badge of silver worth more than gold

The sweat and tears it took to be

A part of the Airborne Infantry

Fort Benning, Georgia, was the place

That made the man pray for grace

For many would try but would have to pack

For the weak would not survive the fury of the Blackhat.

But those who make it will walk proud

With their heads high in the clouds

For there's no other joy that can bring

The pride of earning the Silver Wings.

Sister

As pure as a pearl on the ocean floor

Or the fresh fallen snow on a winter morn.

As innocent as the dew on the ground

She's God's gift to us and we are glad she is around.

A part of a family that cannot be replaced

And life is not the same if we don't see her face.

For she holds a special place in our heart

And we will be together forever until death do us part.

Some Gave All

From Valley Forge to Afghanistan

We fought for Freedom and made a stand

But Glory comes at such a cost

Some Warriors returned and some were lost.

America has never failed,

To fight the battle and then prevail.

Now back at home where mothers weep

Daddy's wonder and children sleep.

For the sons and brothers who answered the call

For most gave some, but some gave all.

Sorrow Follows Me

My Life is filled with sorrows and pain

A constant life of wearing chains

But I will never be set free

Because sorrow follows me.

People I have loved the most

Have all died and turned to ghosts

But will we ever meet again?

I say no because of sin.

I guess it is not meant to be

Because sorrow follows me.

So as I live this sorry life

Filled with heartache, woe and strife

I know there has to be a way

Then maybe I can look and see

That sorrow has stopped following me.

Spring Wedding

When the wind blows love into the air

Two hearts will dream of the love they'll share.

For life goes by so very fast

And we search the world for a love that will last.

Then comes the day when you finally meet

And you thank God above for this love so sweet.

For a Boy and Girl start their life anew

With a simple vow, golden rings and a sweet "I do".

Now you're both so happy you just want to sing

And your first night together is full of dreams.

Of the greatest day of your life

The one where you became Husband and Wife.

Swift as the Wind

They roam the prairies of God's promised land.

Their beauty and elegance is seen in the sand.

With speed and grace they gallop along

And poets have written in story and song.

White men have captured and Indians ride

These creatures of nature work hard to survive.

The mustang has been here since man started sin

And they continue to be as swift as the wind.

Thanks for the Memories

A child was born on the 29th of May 1903

Who would bring joy and laughter to you and me

From Vaudeville, Radio and the movie screen

He brought happiness and laughter wherever he was seen

Like the road trips, he took to dance and sing

With Dorothy Lamore and his good friend Bing

Or the people he charmed with grace and elegance

To include world Dignitaries and U.S. Presidents

His smile would light up many faces

In far away lands and war torn places

From WWII to Desert Storm

He gave us a piece of home with his humor and charm

For one hundred years, God allowed him to stay

To bring joy and happiness in his own special way

But now he's gone and we must cope

Thanks for the Memories Mr. Bob Hope.

The Civil War

There was a time in history as no other

When America's sons fought each other

For the right to keep a man in chains

The South fought the North and caused such pain

It started one day in the South Carolina State

And the United States started her fate

It took four long and terrible years

Of death, killing, and so many tears

To realize our mistakes and shame

And give America back her name

So on a warm and sunny day

General Lee and Grant made their way

To Appomattox Courthouse where they would meet

To sign the treaty so bitter sweet

For now was the time to heal the sore

And learn from the history of the Civil War.

The Second World War

At Pearl Harbor, Hawaii on a warm day

Families woke and children played

But on this day their lives would change

For the Japanese were coming in planes

To bomb and destroy the American Fleet

And knock the super power off her feet

The hell that followed was beyond belief

For they killed and mangled, then left like a thief

Oh, we would not let them die in vain

So we started a war to win our freedom again

Yes, it was time to settle the score

So that's how we entered "The Second World War".

The Vietnam War

In Southeast Asia there is a place

Where American's would fight to save a race

In jungle terrain so thick and hot

We fought in places where others would not

So far away from family and friends

We prayed to God to make it all end

But this conflict was more than just a war

For it caused many battles on our own home shore

Young people protested for what they believe

While many would die and families would grieve

Unlike other wars where soldiers would fight

This was controlled by politics and that just wasn't right

But many years have passed and I am still sore

For the ways our Veterans were treated after "The Vietnam War".

Things Change

The moon will set, the sun will rise

Our whole world is one surprise

Changes are good and full of hope

For our life when we find it hard to cope

Seasons will change; Summer to Winter, Spring to Fall

People also change; happy to sad, short to tall

As the world turns, things have changed

Causing our lives to be re-arranged

We can't stop the constant process of life

Just go with the flow and take it all in strife.

Three Strikes You're Out

At the end of a town there is a ball field

Where children have played for many years

The bases are paper and the grass is high

But to them is doesn't matter, they always get by

The game is older than the kids that play

They love it so much they're there everyday

So the spirit continues and that's why they shout

One, two, three strikes you're out.

Tiger

He stalks his prey with anticipation

Waiting to make his move without hesitation

He's not king of the jungle, he's just a daddy.

But this Tiger strikes with a golf ball and caddy

Tiger has played since he was a cub

Who masters the game with each stroke of his club

Wherever he goes, his loyal fans follow

To see the competition get chewed up and swallowed

This young Tiger gets better each day

For he plays the game in a whole new way

Feared by competitors but loved by fans

He holds his subjects in the palm of his hands

Very few people play the game as good

As the one and only "Tiger" Woods.

U.S. Marines

Standing tall and looking good

Just the way they know they should.

Death before dishonor is the battle cry

And the motto Semper Fi is what they live by.

The few, the proud, is their claim to fame

But only the strong will earn the name.

Their dress blue uniform is neat and clean

Causing people to stare where ever they're seen.

A history that includes land, air and sea

That's why they are called U.S. Marines.

Violence in the Street

Every night on the evening news

People are hurt or die with the blues.

We try so hard to win the fight

But society won't help and that's just not right.

Mom and Dad's, children and friends,

W're all affected it just never ends.

But everything continues, it's all just the same

Bodies in the streets without any name.

So until we can stop and finally meet

We will never stop the violence in the streets.

We Never Agree

A constant life of battle and fight

We never agree or care who is right

Heartache and sorrow, loneliness and strife

I can't keep living this whirlwind life

Why can't we just get along?

It's the same old story of what went wrong

So, I must leave and get away

For I can't live this day by day

I must go now so I can be free

No matter what we do, we never agree.

Where Eagles Soar

High in the mountains where beauty is bound

Lies a creature whose legend is left to be found.

With elegance and grace she soars through the air

Absorbing her kingdom without any care.

Though many have tried to steal her away

The place where she soars is still there today.

One of God's greatest gifts for us to behold

There are still many stories left to be told.

The legend lives on and you can be sure

The greatest beauty on earth is where Eagles soar.

Wolves

Deep in the woods or the frozen plateau

Lives the wolf that we know by the story that's told

His teeth sharp as razors and fur soft as silk

He prowls through the land with the grace of an elk

Indians worship and men try to kill

But the wolf has prevailed and is here with us still.

One of nature's great mysteries so cunning and wise

He'll be here forever, for us to behold in our lives.

So when the wolves howl and the full moon is high

It's their way of saying Goodnight and Goodbye.

The Wrestler

The shadow of a man can be seen on the wall

Concentration on moves that will earn him a fall.

He's known as a wrestler, he works hard at his trade

And his blood, sweat and tears make everything okay.

When he wins, he gets glory and it makes him feel good

But if he loses, he knows he didn't do what he should.

So this is the story of a sport that is pure

And that is the life of a man called a wrestler.